A Gift From:

Millie

To:

Claudia

And now these three remain: faith, hope and love.
But the greatest of these is love.

Mothers Day
_2001_

Keeping Love Alive

Zondervan

BOK4015

*I*f I speak in the tongues of men and of angels, but have not love, I am only a resounding gong or a clanging cymbal. If I have the gift of prophecy and can fathom all mysteries and all knowledge, and if I have a faith that can move mountains, but have not love, I am nothing. If I give all I possess to the poor and surrender my body to the flames, but have not love, I gain nothing.

Love is patient, love is kind. It does not envy, it does not boast, it is not proud. It is not rude, it is not self-seeking, it is not easily angered, it keeps no record of wrongs. Love does not delight in evil but rejoices with the truth. It always protects, always trusts, always hopes, always perseveres. Love never fails.

—1 Corinthians 13:1-8

Keeping Love Alive

$\mathcal{R}$omance isn't reserved just for the young, and neither is it reserved for the bedroom. Being affectionate, thoughtful, and kind at other times will spill over into your love life. We all like to be nurtured and cherished. Phone calls, notes that say, "I love you," cooking your mate's favorite dish, giving a bouquet of flowers, holding hands, a peck on the cheek, a wink across the room, and saying loving and endearing things to each other will add romance to your relationship.

—David and Claudia Arp

$\mathcal{L}$ove is the ultimate good. It lifts us outside ourselves. Love sees beyond the normal range of human vision — over walls of resentment and barriers of betrayal. Love rises above the petty demands and conflicts of life and inspires our spirit to transcend who we are tempted to settle for: decent, but merely mediocre. Love aims higher. Unencumbered by self-absorption, love charms us to reach our ideal. Love allures us with a hint of what might be possible.

—Les and Leslie Parrott

To form a forever relationship, you will need a Love-centered marriage. The love you have at the beginning with its intensely personal quality of belonging and possessing fluctuates because it is fed by feelings, and feelings change, especially if needs and desires are not being met. But the God of Love has made his own love available to each of us. That love, which the Bible calls agape, never changes. It is unconditional and does not depend on a person's behavior. It goes right on showing kindness to the beloved, no matter what, because it is controlled not by our emotions, but by our will. The ability to love this way is a gift from God through his Son Jesus Christ; his love channeled through us blesses our mate and our marriage.

—Ed Wheat

*G*enuine love doesn't necessarily spring from feelings. Its basis is primarily a concern for the welfare of another. Although the feelings of affection will follow, genuine love is initially an action directed toward fulfilling another person's needs.

—*Gary Smalley*

*H*ouses and wealth are inherited from parents, but a prudent wife is from the Lord.

—*Proverbs 19:14*

*L*ike separate strings of a lute that quiver with the same music, there is beauty in a marriage that respects the individuality of its partners. In an interdependent marriage, joy is doubled, and sorrow is cut in half.

—*Les and Leslie Parrott*

Tips for Loving Her

Write her a love poem for her birthday.

Give her a foot massage.

Tell her how attractive she is.

Pray for her.

Surprise her with breakfast in bed.

Hold her hand in public.

Learn to enjoy shopping.

Fix dinner for her.

Value what she says.

Tell her how proud you are of her.

*L*ove without intimacy is only a hormonal illusion. One cannot desire another person over the long haul without really knowing that person.

Intimacy has a "best friend" or "soul mate" quality about it. We all want someone who knows us better than anyone else—and still accepts us. And we want someone who holds nothing back from us, someone who trusts us with personal secrets. Intimacy fills our heart's deepest longings for closeness and acceptance.

People who have successfully built an intimate relationship know its power and comfort, but they also know that taking the emotional risks that allow intimacy to happen isn't easy. Without careful nurturing, intimacy withers.

—Les and Leslie Parrott

$\mathcal{R}$oger and I have found that we have stayed more con- nected in our current roles than when we maintained more traditional roles. We talk and pray by telephone each night that I am out of town, and when I get home, we always have a date planned to go to a movie or out to dinner alone or with other couples. And because I travel often, we have accrued travel miles that provide a yearly family vacation with other families we have met through my speaking engagements, widening our circle of friends.

—*Dr. Roger and Becky Tirabassi*

$\mathcal{L}$ove one another. As I have loved you, so you must love one another.

—*John 13:34*

$\mathcal{O}$f all the little expressions of love—a box of chocolates, a handwritten poem, or a bouquet of handpicked wildflowers— I think my favorite is a good old-fashioned kiss on the lips. Whether it be the gratuitous kind that comes with greeting my husband after a day at work or his surprising ambush kiss while standing in line at the grocery, I always feel especially loved when Les gives me a simple kiss.

—*Les and Leslie Parrott*

I'm a big believer in marriage. I have never seen happier, more deeply satisfied people than men and women who have made their marriages work. But neither have I met many people in highly successful marriages who got there without an enormous expenditure of energy and determination. There were times when they simply had to be "willful." Virtually every successful marriage requires all kinds of willpower. Sometimes issues arise and the partners don't have the necessary skills to manage them. They essentially have two choices: give up and run away, or get about the task of developing the required skills. Partners with willpower always adopt the second alternative. They wouldn't think of giving up. They are ready to go to work on the problem, ready to do whatever they must to keep their marriage healthy for a lifetime.

—*Dr. Neil Clark Warren*

*T*he bonds of matrimony are like any other bonds, they mature slowly.

—*Peter De Vries*

*W*hatever love is, it is not easy to pin down, for love is a strange mixture of opposites. It includes affection and anger, excitement and boredom, stability and change, restriction and freedom. Love's ultimate paradox is two beings becoming one, yet remaining two.

—*Les and Leslie Parrott*

*S*howing appreciation not only demonstrates faithfulness to your partner, it builds more loving faithfulness in your own heart. It is amazing how we tend to believe our own spoken words. So be careful what you say and always speak positively.

—*Ed Wheat*

*W*ives, submit to your husbands, as is fitting in the Lord. Husbands, love your wives and do not be harsh with them.

—*Colossians 3:18,19*

Keeping Love Alive

Ideas for Dating

*Go out for coffee and reminisce about a date you had that
neither of you will forget.*

Visit a museum.

*Go shopping and buy a Christmas tree
ornament for each other.*

Stay home, eat popcorn, and watch your favorite video.

Plant flowers or a tree together.

*Look through each other's childhood pictures.
Pick out the favorite one of your spouse and share
why you chose that one.*

Go bowling together.

Eat out at an Italian restaurant for dinner.

See a romantic movie together.

Take a day off to be together.

$\mathcal{L}$iving happily ever after only works when you make it work. When you take the raw materials of marriage—the good and the bad that you've brought together as persons— to design, create, and build a lasting bond, the result is an enduring and meaningful sense of genuine fulfillment. If, on the other hand, you are counting on the magic of marriage to make you happy, the relationship will leave you crushed, lonely, feeling like a failure, and resigned to your despair.

The habit of happiness is an inside job. If you find the right attitude in spite of atmospheric conditions, if you program your mind with positive impulses, and if you adjust to things beyond your control, you will discover that living happily ever after need not be a myth.

—*Les and Leslie Parrott*

$\mathcal{I}$f there is anything better
than to be loved
it is loving.

—*Anonymous*

Keeping Love Alive

_If_ you want your marital relationship to deepen, it is very important that you learn to be flexible. I believe there is nothing as important to you or your family as a good, loving relationship with your husband. Your flexibility can make your husband feel really special and can keep that "spark" in your relationship. When he comes home and sees that you are willing to set aside your schedule for an unrushed conversation, he feels valued and loved. Your schedule is important, I realize. However, you need to maintain a balance by being able to set aside your priorities from time to time to pay special attention to your husband and his needs. That's genuine love.

—*Gary Smalley*

*M*arital success comes through daily struggles. Marriage is made up of the daily grind—the little things like making unselfish choices and forgiving each other help to build a healthy marriage. Little steps, if taken in good faith, can turn the tide.

—David and Claudia Arp

*L*ove and faithfulness meet together; righteousness and peace kiss each other.

—Psalm 85:10

*C*ommunication is the lifeblood of marriage.

—Les and Leslie Parrott

*R*emember that when you listen to your partner, you are showing love. You are giving your partner the message, "What you have to say to me is important because you are important."

—Ed Wheat

If your marriage is coming in a distant second or third or fourth behind a lot of other "priorities," you need to grapple with reality. And reality says that if you don't start doing things differently, you have an excellent chance of becoming one more statistic, one more small part of the giant national average that says a marriage lasts some seven years and is gone.

In a word, you must prioritize within, and that means your spouse must come first. When your marriage comes first, everything else falls into its proper place.

For any couple—particularly the overly busy, hard-driving husbands and wives who are trying to juggle career and family—there is more reason than ever to seek refuge in each other, to have some times for yourselves. To keep your family together, you must start at the bottom—at the foundation of it all—your marriage relationship. Finding time for each other can be done—if you both really want to.

—*Dr. Kevin Leman*

Keeping Love Alive

$\mathcal{L}$aughing at your partner's dumbest jokes, playing games or sports together, enjoying each other's idiosyncrasies, bragging about your better half, and uplifting your spouse with your smile or hug are encouragements every person needs, yet often in the marriage relationship they get ignored. Fun, humor, affirmation, and encouragement are part of the friendship that a spouse should provide. Committing to a "best friend" relationship with your spouse sets the stage for intimacy.

—Dr. Roger and Becky Tirabassi

$\mathcal{L}$ove must be sincere. Hate what is evil; cling to what is good.

—Romans 12:9

$\mathcal{C}$ommunication skills are important to learn—no doubt about it—but they fall flat without love. They turn into tools of manipulation. "You're just doing that thing our counselor said to do" is the response a new technique often elicits in the absence of love. So before you try to tune up your talk, overhaul your heart. Allow love to seize every word, every syllable. Invite love to lay claim to your conversation.

—Les and Leslie Parrott

Listen to Him

Listen to how he feels about his greatest pleasures in life.

Listen to how he feels about his most difficult
weekly challenge.

Listen to his favorite jokes.

Listen to how he feels about his least attractive feature.

Listen to how he feels about television sports.

Listen to how he feels about his greatest weakness.

Listen to how he feels about his greatest hope
for the future.

Listen to how he feels about his childhood.

Listen to how he feels about his greatest strength.

Listen to how he feels about his job.

Keeping Love Alive

Forgiveness is a key element in healthy long-term marriages. Forgiveness is the oil that lubricates a love relationship, and it's an oil we need daily. Forgiveness is not a one-time event; it's an attitude of wanting to partner with your spouse in spite of his or her imperfections and irritations.

Is there something right now that disappoints you about your mate or your relationship? Grievances can range in intensity from habitually leaving the TV on to having illicit affairs. No matter where your disappointments and hurts fall on the continuum, you must decide to forgive your spouse and move beyond these grievances before you can work on developing an exuberant, growing marriage.

Remember, forgiveness begins with a simple decision, a simple act of the will. We are to forgive as God has forgiven us. It is not dependent upon our spouse asking for our forgiveness or even acknowledging he or she has done anything wrong.

—David and Claudia Arp

*T*he fulfillment of love hinges on closeness, sharing, communication, honesty, and support. As one heart given in exchange for another, marriage provides the deepest and most radical expression of intimacy.

—*Les and Leslie Parrott*

*M*ake it a point to share your feelings, but not in such a way that your partner feels criticized. Encourage your partner to share his feelings and respond to them lovingly. Give him or her the gift of sympathy and empathy. This is one way to teach each other to give what you both are longing for.

—*Ed Wheat*

*D*o everything in love.

—*1 Corinthians 16:14*

Keeping Love Alive

"*I* will love you when times are good or bad. I will cherish you even if I am upset with you. I will honor you at all times." Every couple can profit from saying these simple words to each other every day. The more each person can find new and creative ways to swear this commitment, the better. For instance, some part of it can be put into a lunch sack, engraved inside a bracelet, scribbled on a refrigerator note in the morning, contained in a love letter, or written in the sky above a football game.

The idea is to recite this vow over and over so that when the rocky times come, as they inevitably will, the commitment to love, honor, and cherish will trigger new ideas in the brain about how to hold the marriage together.

—Dr. Neil Clark Warren

*M*arriages can never be perfect because people are not perfect. Being human, every bride and groom has faults as well as virtues. We are at times gloomy, cranky, selfish, or unreasonable. We are a mixture of generous, altruistic feelings combined with self-seeking aims, petty vanities, and ambitions. We unite love and courage with selfishness and fear. Marriage is an alloy of gold and tin. If we expect more than this, we are doomed to disappointment.

—Les and Leslie Parrott

*H*e who finds a wife finds what is good and receives favor from the Lord.

—Proverbs 18:22

*T*here is no right or wrong time to praise your wife. She'll love it when you're alone or when you're with the children and friends. Make sure you don't limit your praise to public or private times. If you only praise her in public, she might suspect you're showing off for your friends. If you only praise her in private, she may feel you're embarrassed about doing it.

—Gary Smalley

Encourage Each Other

*Make out two sets of New Year's resolutions.
One for yourself, one for your spouse. Then compare.*

Pray for each other everyday.

Write your spouse a note. The key word is "Appreciate."

*Encourage your spouse today in something
he or she must do.*

*Write your spouse a brief love letter for the month.
Include these words: "thoughtful," "caring," and "best."*

Do not criticize in front of others.

*Stick by your spouse at a party and draw
him or her into the conversation.*

Compliment each other.

Freely discuss your opinions of the headline news.

Give advice in a loving way when he/she asks for it.

*H*usbands place surprising importance on having their wives as recreational companions. The commercial caricature of men out in the wilderness, cold beer in hand, saying, "It doesn't get any better then this," is false. It can get a lot better than that when a wife joins her husband in a shared activity that he enjoys.

Don't allow you and your partner to drift apart because you can't find something enjoyable to do together. I have seen too many marriages fizzle because a wife didn't use her creative energies to build enjoyable moments of fun and relaxation with her husband. Make a careful list of recreational interests your husband enjoys. Next, circle those activities that you might find somewhat pleasurable. You can probably find a good half-dozen activities that you can enjoy with your husband. Your next task is to schedule these activities into your recreational time together.

If you learn to meet your husband's need for recreational companionship, you will discover that you are not only husband and wife, but best friends too.

—*Les and Leslie Parrott*

$\mathcal{A}$t the touch of love everyone
becomes a poet.

—*Plato*

*O*ver the last two decades, marriage specialists have researched the ingredients of a happy marriage. As a result, we know more about building a successful marriage today than ever before. For example, happily married couples will have:

Healthy expectations of marriage

A realistic concept of love

A positive attitude and outlook toward life

The ability to communicate their feelings

An understanding and acceptance of their gender differences

The ability to make decisions and settle arguments

A common spiritual foundation and goal

Every couple should be aware of these issues before (and after) they marry. Taking the time to understand these issues is like investing in an insurance policy against divorce.

—Les and Leslie Parrott

Keeping Love Alive

*T*hrough trial and error, and deep commitment to each other, we made three fundamental decisions that helped our relationship grow more secure and intimate. We decided that to stay close to each other we had to do the following:

Spend quality and quantity time together!

Never quit!

Become each other's best friend and biggest encourager!

—Dr. Roger and Becky Tirabassi

A wife of noble character is her husband's crown, but a disgraceful wife is like decay in his bones.

—Proverbs 12:4

*H*ealthy long-term marriages have staying power, because they are held together from within. Competent couples invest time and energy in building and maintaining a positive relationship with each other.

—David and Claudia Arp

*I*f the husband's responsibility can be summarized in one phrase: Love your wife! Your calling as a wife can also be summed up in a few words: Respond to your husband! You must remember there is only one way to convince your husband that you love him, and that is by your loving response—a response that he can see, hear, touch, feel, and enjoy on a daily basis, a response that includes the physical, but also touches every aspect of his life. This is your contribution to a love-filled, lasting marriage. Many wives who have enjoyed lifelong love affairs with their husbands say that this is their secret of success.

—*Ed Wheat*

Keeping Love Alive

*O*ne of the great illusions of our age is that love is self-sustaining. It is not. Marriage expert David Mace says, "Love must be fed and nurtured . . . first and foremost it demands time." Studies indicate that marital happiness is highly correlated with the amount of time spent together. We often encourage busy couples to schedule lunches together or "no-television nights" at home. Heart-to-heart talks don't happen on the go.

—*Les and Leslie Parrott*

*W*hen your spouse makes a statement, you can follow by saying, "What I hear you saying is . . . ." At that point, your spouse can say, "Yes, that's what I meant" or "No, that's not what I meant at all!" Keep the communication cycle going until you both agree that what your spouse said is what you heard. This will greatly help your communication.

—*David and Claudia Arp*

Talk Together

Talk about what each of you thinks is "romantic."

Agree upon two foods that will never be served at home.

Decide on one special thing each person could do for his or her in-laws.

Negotiate who will shop for which relatives at Christmas.

Decide together approximately how much time you need to reserve for just the two of you to be together in an average week.

Decide on a night each of you can go out with friends this week.

Negotiate what your next major purchase should be.

Suggest one book each person wants the other to read.

Negotiate times for each of you to exercise or play sports.

Discuss the amount of time it takes for both of you to do the weekend chores. Divide the chores in such a way that both of you agree is fair.

$\mathcal{P}$rotecting your spouse's confidence is critical to building a trustworthy marriage. Unfortunately, some couples become contaminated by gossip. Not shop gossip. Not party gossip. But gossip behind a partner's back about the state of the relationship. "I probably shouldn't even be telling you this but..."

Think of the remarkable energy that would be restored to a marriage if the partners "gossiped" about good things instead of bad. If, for example, a wife confided in a friend how sweet her husband was to clean up the kitchen. If you are ever snared by the grip of gossip in your own marriage, consider gabbing about the good. Leave the secrets at home and never betray a confidence.

—Les and Leslie Parrot

*E*xamine your typical schedules, and pick times when you can focus on each other's feelings, concerns, and interests. This could be at dinner, but it may work better just before going to sleep. Try lying in each other's arms and talking about how you feel—what is causing joy, what is causing anxiety and concern. Make it a time to be open and honest, but avoid attacking and complaining.

—Dr. Kevin Leman

*W*hen forgiveness is truly necessary, forgive as quickly as you can, because forgiving has two good results: The first is your own release, and the second is the possibility of reconciliation between you and your mate.

—Lewis Smedes

*B*ut the fruit of the Spirit is love, joy, peace, patience, kindness, goodness, faithfulness, gentleness and self-control.

—Galatians 5:22

*W*e suggest that you have a daily time when you simply touch base and share with each other. Perhaps a tea time or coffee time each morning would be a good format for a couple time. Many couples benefit from their regular times when they record their feelings and thoughts in a journal for ten minutes and then share what they have written with each other and talk about it. One couple we know cleans up the kitchen together each morning after breakfast. While it only takes a couple of minutes, it's when they touch base. Using whatever works best for you, find a way to touch emotionally each day. Your marriage will be the benefactor!

—*David and Claudia Arp*

*M*en have a tough time realizing that offering a listening ear is all a woman needs at times—or a comforting hug, a loving statement like "You are hurting, aren't you?" or "You are under a lot of pressure, aren't you?" Listening to your wife talk without offering quick solutions is the only way to meet her need to be known.

—*Les and Leslie Parrott*

*W*e acknowledge our need to live with a life-long mate, but we find that living with them can be difficult. Our belief is that living with them can also be a joy if we have realistic expectations, prepare for our inevitable struggles and make the necessary adjustments for our differing personalities and needs.

—*Dr. Roger and Becky Tirabassi*

Tips for Loving Him

Give him a foot massage.

Surprise him with breakfast in bed.

Give him a Saturday off.

Buy a magazine he would enjoy reading.

Send him a fax.

Don't mention his hair loss—he already knows.

Buy yourself something sexy—for him.

Say you are sorry.

Write "I love you" on the steamy mirror when he's in the shower.

Make him laugh.

$\mathcal{M}$illions of couples are robbed of happiness because one of the partners has developed a negative mind-set, blaming their unhappiness on things their spouse does or doesn't do. It's one of the worst mistakes a person can make in marriage. We often hear statements in counseling like: "Her comments hurt me!" or "He makes me so angry." In reality, remarks and comments do not hurt or upset people; people can only upset themselves. Of course, being upset is a natural reaction to something we dislike, but that reaction can serve as a trigger for a more constructive, positive response.

When we recognize where the control resides—in ourselves and not in external events—we are able to reinterpret upsetting events and develop a positive attitude.

—Les and Leslie Parrott

*I*mmature love says: "I love you because I need you." Mature love says: "I need you because I love you."

—*Erich Fromm*

Tips for Staying in Love

Concentrate on building an intimate relationship.

Nurture each other emotionally.

Touch lovingly, share thoughts and feelings.

Spend private time together so that you can continue to feel secure and at home in each other's presence.

Avoid the negatives that could change the way you see each other. Live in an atmosphere of approval, and forgive quickly and generously.

Live out your commitment to one another in such a way that strong links of trust are established and maintained.

Build your marriage on a solid biblical base. Always think and talk in "forever" terms.

—*Ed Wheat*

Keeping Love Alive

*A*sk any couple who has been happily married for fifty years if their love life was a cakewalk. You'll be hard pressed to find one. Sure, many seasoned couples focus their memories on the positive side, but every lifelong couple who can look back over the decades together has endured tough times. You can be sure of that. And you can be sure of one other thing: They persevered, not because of legal or social constraints, but because love endures to the last.

—*Les and Leslie Parrott*

*W*hat kind of praise would you like to hear from your boss? Try a little of it on your wife. You may say, "Well, I don't need too much praise. I'm secure in my job, and I really don't need it." Then interview some of those who work with you to see how they would appreciate being praised. Some of their ideas might work with your wife. Also, ask your wife what kind of praise she likes to hear.

—*Gary Smalley*

*W*hen two people enjoy partner-centered sex, their love-making is never repetitive, boring, or mechanical. Partner-centered sex depends on your motivation, for it will require careful study of your partner to learn what brings pleasure to him or her. Becoming sensitive to your partner's needs and desires, implied or stated, means listening with your whole being to that person. It involves reading body language, observing even the slightest word or gesture and discerning what it means. You will lovingly put forth effort to discover your partner's wishes, to find out what "feels good." You will learn your partner's likes, dislikes, what parts of his or her body are most erotic, and the ways of loving that evoke a response at that particular moment.

—*Ed Wheat*

Keeping Love Alive

$\mathcal{E}$very couple tells little white lies to one another in an attempt to be more loving. If we don't like our partner's cooking, for example, we might say, "Oh, it's wonderful." A little lie won't hurt our relationship, will it? Wrong. The tragedy of most small deceptions is that they mushroom, ultimately creating a cloud of distrust that hovers over a relationship.

—Les and Leslie Parrott

$\mathcal{L}$et love and faithfulness never leave you; bind them around your neck, write them on the tablet of your heart.

—Proverbs 3:3

$\mathcal{M}$ake it a practice to give each other your complete attention when you talk together. If you only half-listen, you will only half-hear and that's not good enough. Try to listen with your heart as well as your ears to hear what the other is really saying and feeling. Remember that "the human heart holds more than speech does."

—Ed Wheat

Just for Fun

Go for a walk in the park. Take your camera and get snapshots of each other.

Write your spouse a brief love letter. Spray your favorite perfume on the paper to give it a special touch.

Go to an amusement park.

Pack a little basket of your favorite snacks and watch fireworks.

Go to a nearby park and play on the swings.

Play miniature golf without competing.

Go to the zoo and imitate the animals.

Start laughing and see who can laugh the longest.

Take bread to a nearby pond and feed the fish.

Find a good taffy recipe and make it together. Have fun pulling the taffy!

Keeping Love Alive

$\mathcal{P}$hysical contact is a powerful means of communicating and a gentle and supportive way to nourish the spirit and convey positive emotions. Imagine for a moment that you come home from a tough day, feeling tense, tired, and irritable—but then your partner wraps you in his or her arms and gives you a loving squeeze. That hug causes a rise in hemoglobin, a substance in the red blood cells that transports energizing oxygen throughout your body. Incredible, that gentle hug or even a soft caress can cause a speeding heart to quiet, soaring blood pressure to drop, and severe pain to ease.

Given its potent impact on our lives, it's no wonder that touch is known as the "mother of the sense." There is simply no better way to communicate the idea that "you are not alone," or "I love you." So the next time you're at a loss for words, remember, touching may be the best way of speaking to your partner.

—Les and Leslie Parrott

Keeping Love Alive

*C*riticism may seem fairly harmless, even "constructive" under certain circumstances. Yet it has the potential to bring about the slow, painful death of a love relationship: when criticism drips unchecked, love dies by inches. The deadly destroyer of marriage, criticism should be replaced by encouragement and edifying.

—Ed Wheat

*C*ommitment creates a small island of certainty in the swirling waters of uncertainty. As the mooring of marriage, commitment secures love for our partner when passion burns low and when turbulent times and fierce impulses overtake us.

—Les and Leslie Parrott

*B*ut you must return to your God; maintain love and justice, and wait for your God always.

—Hosea 12:6

*M*ore than anything else, what gets in the way of getting along is self-centeredness that seems reasonable. God does his deepest work in making us more truly loving when we more clearly see how utterly ugly our selfishness is.

Getting along with each other requires that we stop making excuses for all the selfish things we do. And if our tendency toward self-justification can be weakened, perhaps then we will more easily recognize our anger when it's there, call it wrong, and experience the thrill of Christ's forgiveness and the power of his cleansing. We're not condemned, and we're empowered to love.

—*Dr. Larry Crabb*

*T*his is my prayer: that your love may abound more and more in knowledge and depth of insight, so that you may be able to discern what is best and may be pure and blameless until the day of Christ.

—*Philippians 1: 9,10*

*K*indness sets aside the fear that we will be exploited. It relinquishes self-focus and is energized by the needs of another. Kindness causes us to pause from our own pursuits in order to augment somebody else's life. Make no mistake about it: Once we remove kindness from a loving heart it is only a matter of time before the heart atrophies and love is lost altogether.

—*Les and Leslie Parrott*

Listen to Her

Listen to how she feels about the amount of time
you spend with her.

Listen to how she feels about in-laws.

Listen as she recalls her best Christmas memory.

Listen to how she feels about your sex life.

Listen to how she feels about her parents.

Listen to how she feels about the amount of time the two of
you actually spend talking to each other.

Listen to how she feels about the amount of time you spend
talking with the children.

Listen to how she feels about the family budget.

Listen to how she feels about working or not working
outside of the home.

Listen to how she feels about planning fun times.

$\mathcal{R}$oger and I backed up our general decision to never quit with some specific decisions that also helped ensure the success of our marriage. We decided to

talk when we didn't want to,

make love when we didn't necessarily feel like it,

save when we wanted to spend,

work when we would rather play,

and go to church when we felt like sleeping in.

They were and are hard decisions! (We still have to make them!) They are seldom easy or fun, but they are essential to an effective marriage.

—Dr. Roger and Becky Tirabassi

$\mathcal{A}$ woman loves to find hidden notes—in her jewelry box, the silver drawer, the medicine cabinet. Search for ways to praise your wife. The possibilities are endless.

—Gary Smalley

$\mathcal{L}$ife has taught us that love does not consist in gazing at each other but in looking outward together in the same direction.

—*Antoine de Saint-Exupery*

*W*ithin a marriage, an apology to your partner that is sincerely meant is much more than a civility—it can be a powerful tool for resolving issues and strengthening your relationship.

True apologies in marriage can happen only when partners come to understand accountability. This is another way of saying that each of you must take responsibility for your own behavior, acknowledge your partner's point of view, and at times own up to things about yourself you don't like. Finally, it may mean making changes.

All couples need a healing mechanism, a way to run a new page in marriage, and knowing how and when to say you're sorry can make a big difference. An apology may not be a literal "I'm sorry"; it may be giving gifts, sharing an evening out, or simply taking a quiet walk together. The point is that a sincere apology, whatever its form, leaves the couple with a renewed closeness and a relieved feeling that all is well.

—Les and Leslie Parrott

Keeping Love Alive

*H*ere are a few nonverbal ways to show your husband how important he is:

Be attentive to his concerns when he comes home.

Look as attractive as possible when he comes home.

Prepare appetizing meals.

Show interest and ask questions about his job, activities, problems, achievements.

Listen attentively by focusing your eyes on him.

Don't make him compete with the TV, the dishes, or even the children when he's trying to talk to you.

—Gary Smalley

*L*oving couples use every opportunity to boost each other in front of other people and to cast each other in the best light—much as they did in their courting days, when they wanted their friends and family to like their new love. They say things like, "Sarah just got a promotion, but she won't tell you that." Or, "Rick may not mention it, but he secured a huge grant for his company this week." Loving couples praise one another in private and in public. They tell each other's stories of accomplishment.

—Les and Leslie Parrott

*A*dd some adventure. Try a little spontaneity. If you always make love in the evening, try mornings. Call in late for work and grab a couple of hours with each other while you are fresh. Plan a middle-of-the-day rendezvous. One couple, who both work downtown, took a picnic basket to work and met at a downtown motel on their lunch break. Another couple, on a more austere budget, met during their afternoon break in their car in the parking garage for hugs and kisses. Go on and brainstorm. You're only limited by your imagination! Try some variety in when and where you make love. Remember, variety can be the spice of life. Be explorers.

—*David and Claudia Arp*

*E*verything a wife can do for her husband comes under these three ways of loving: A wife loves her husband and meets his needs by

 (1) helping him;

 (2) responding to him emotionally and physically; and

 (3) respecting him.

—Ed Wheat

*E*very thriving marriage is grounded in passion, intimacy, and commitment. Cultivating these three elements will help you successfully navigate the stages of love and make it last a lifetime.

—Les and Leslie Parrott

*L*et us consider how we may spur one another on toward love and good deeds.

—Hebrews 10:24

Just Do It

Begin each day with a hug and a kiss.

Don't miss a birthday or special day.
Write them on a calendar.

Decorate Christmas cookies together.

Hang her picture in your office.

Share a hug and a kiss at midnight on New Year's Eve.

Convince him to do something silly —just with you.

Write your spouse a note using "Thoughtful" as a key word.

Make a taco salad together for dinner.

Go through all your clothes and give away any clothes
you do not wear anymore.

Both of you put the kids to bed this evening. Be creative
and tell a bedtime story that the two of you have made
up together.

Brag about your spouse to other people behind his/her back.

Keeping Love Alive

*W*ithout hope, marriage becomes a living hell. Dante tells us that the sign that hangs over the entrance to hell reads, "Abandon hope, ye who enter here." That's why love always hopes, even in some of the most hopeless situations. An alcoholic husband who has turned his wife's everyday life into a hellish nightmare strains hope, but yet it can survive. A wife who has secretly maxed out every credit card and driven her husband into debt without his knowledge pushes the limits of hope, but yet it can live. As long as hope survives so does a glimmer of love. Hope enables love to coexist with life's inevitable pain.

—*Les and Leslie Parrott*

*W*hen you initiate sex from time to time, use imagination to make the bedroom and your appearance as inviting as possible. Perfume, candlelight, gentle words, and a soft touch are just a few of the ways you can add creativity to the occasion.

Another way to make the occasion more fulfilling for you and your husband is for each of you to concentrate on meeting each other's sexual needs. I have found that a selfless, giving attitude contributes most to sexual enjoyment. A man's greatest fulfillment comes when he puts his whole heart into stimulating his wife and bringing her to a climactic experience. At the same time, a woman is most fulfilled when she concentrates on meeting her husband's needs. Selfish sex does nothing but remove the potential for maximum pleasure. Sex at its best happens when a husband begins to meet his wife's emotional needs on a daily basis. All the techniques and atmosphere in the world can't warm up a neglected wife.

—Gary Smalley

Keeping Love Alive

Sharing life's ultimate meaning with another person is the spiritual call of soul mates, and every couple must answer that call or risk a stunted, underdeveloped marriage. Like yeast in a loaf of bread, spirituality will ultimately determine whether your marriage rises successfully or falls disappointingly flat.

The spiritual dimension of marriage is a practical source of food for marital growth and health. No single factor does more to cultivate oneness and a meaningful sense of purpose in marriage than a shared commitment to spiritual discovery. It is the ultimate hunger of our souls.

—Les and Leslie Parrott

*C*ommunication squeezed in during half-time activities or the commercial breaks will be unsatisfying and, even worse, is the effort to talk something over while the television continues to blare and one partner tries to keep an eye on a favorite program. So forego television, put away the video movies, turn off the radio, and shut down the stereo. Close the doors, get your children (if any) occupied elsewhere, and take the telephone off the hook. Never listen with split attention. The communication system of your marriage deserves the very best.

—Ed Wheat

*B*etter a meal of vegetables where there is love than a fattened calf with hatred.

—Proverbs 15:17

*H*ate stirs up dissension, but love covers over all wrongs.

—Proverbs 10:12

Enjoy Each Other

Make a list of things you do together that bring you joy.
Set dates to do these things together.

Do some form of exercise together today.

Go to a card shop and find romantic cards for each other.
Buy your favorite one and give it with a special note inside.

Put away the laundry together.

Reminisce about the day you met. Try to duplicate
the conversation from your first date.

Have a "just for two" candlelight dinner.

Work together on the lawn or garden.

Go to a Chinese restaurant and try something you
have never eaten before.

Sing songs you liked when you were dating.

*H*ere are a few tips for cultivating politeness in your marriage: Greet each other with an acknowledgment and warm hello, and mark a leaving with a tender good-bye.

When your partner has done a chore, always show appreciation for the job even if the way it was done doesn't meet with your approval (say "Thanks for washing the car" rather than "You missed a spot").

Surround meal times with pleasant conversations. Shut off the TV and pay attention to your mate instead.

Research has shown that it takes only one put-down to undo hours of kindness that you give to your partner. So the most gracious offering of politeness you can give your partner is to avoid put-downs altogether.

—Les and Leslie Parrott

$\mathcal{D}$uty does not have to be dull. Love can make it beautiful and fill it with life.

—*Anonymous*

$\mathcal{W}$hat has happened to all the loveable characteristics that first attracted your husband to you? Perhaps it was your quiet, gentle voice... your gentle spirit... your ability to listen... your vivacious personality... your keen mind... your sense of humor... whatever qualities made the total person to whom he was initially attracted. Have some of them gotten lost through the years? Do you scream for his attention now? Are you too busy to listen to him? Have you lost your sense of humor? If you are to recapture his attention, you must somehow recapture and exhibit those qualities unique to you that first drew him to you.

—Gary Smalley

Keeping Love Alive

*B*e imitators of God, therefore, as dearly loved children and live a life of love, just as Christ loved us and gave himself up for us.

—*Ephesians 5:1,2*

*L*ife is a series of adjustments. Changes are as certain as the seasons. So embrace change. Greet it as a welcomed guest. If you don't like the way things are right now, don't panic—more changes may be just up the road! Grab the initiative and do what you can do to put more fun into your life and more life into your friendship with your spouse. You can start anytime, and it can start with you!

—*David and Claudia Arp*

*R*eal listening involves concentration accompanied by eye contact. When your partner is sharing thoughts and feelings with you, stop what you're doing and respond with your eyes. Stop and make yourself available when you sense your partner may be wanting to talk.

—*Ed Wheat*

To be autonomous is a universal male need. Whenever a man is under stress (an important deadline is approaching, he is under pressure at work, etc.), he requires a little space. At such times he becomes absent-minded, unresponsive, absorbed, and preoccupied. Unlike women, men typically don't want to talk about the situation, they don't want to be held or comforted—not until they have had time to themselves.

Part of the need for autonomy is the man's need to have time to regroup. Some wives complain because their husbands don't immediately talk about their day when they come home from work. They first want to read the paper or water the lawn, anything to clean their mind before engaging in the relationship. It's a male thing. But giving your husband space when he needs it, whether you understand it or not, will gain you a happier husband.

—*Les and Leslie Parrott*

Keeping Love Alive

*H*e who pursues righteousness and love finds life, prosperity and honor.

—Proverbs 21:21

*L*ove must be learned, and learned again and again; there is no end to it.

—Katherine Anne Porter

*I*nsensitivity is like trampling with clodhopper boots over the other person—not out of malice, but ignorance. Love pays the most careful attention to the beloved. Anyone can learn to be sensitive to another person.

—Ed Wheat

*R*emember, it's the little things that really matter. Little things like coming home early and taking her out to dinner at a place she really likes (not the Colonel). Like sending her a note home from the office—handwritten—that says, "I want you to know how much I care. I want you to know how much I appreciate all you do for our family. You do so much for me and for the children. I'm so proud of you."

—Dr. Kevin Leman

Tips for Loving Her

Surprise her with a card or flowers.

Express how much you appreciate her.

Pray for her to enjoy God's best in life.

Let her take a bubble bath while you do the dishes.

Help her finish her goals—hobbies or education.

Get rid of habits that annoy her.

Do not expect a band to play whenever you help with the housecleaning.

Tell her you love her—often.

Give her an engraved plaque assuring her of your lasting love.

Practice common courtesies like holding the door for her, pouring her coffee.

$\mathcal{K}$indness comes from small behaviors. We don't think of big donations or grand contributions as "kind." We call them "generous," "charitable," or "benevolent," but it is the small things we call "kind." Kindness, for example, comes when we turn down our partner's side of the bed before crawling into it ourselves. Kindness comes when we readjust the car seat after driving so our partner doesn't have to. Kindness comes when we load the dishwasher when it's not our turn. Kindness comes from a million small behaviors that enhance the life of the one we love.

—*Les and Leslie Parrott*

*M*ake my joy complete by being like-minded, having the same love, being one in spirit and purpose. Do nothing out of selfish ambition or vain conceit, but in humility consider others better than yourselves.

—Philippians 2:2,3

*D*id you know the word kiss comes from a prehistoric syllable that is believed to be the sound of kissing? However the word originated and whoever named it really doesn't matter to me. I just know that I like kisses. And why shouldn't I? Kisses, according to a Danish saying, are the messengers of love.

—Les and Leslie Parrott

*B*oredom is a tragic waste of the gift of life, and an insult to your partner. Bored people are boring people. Bored people become depressed people. So take action to change your attitude, put the spark back in your marriage, and find joy and excitement in knowing God and discovering how He wants you to serve Him.

—Ed Wheat

Keeping Love Alive

Two of the most important lovemaking skills and romance enhancers are listening with your heart and talking to your spouse while you are loving each other. Your love life may be active, but if it is all action and no talk, you're missing an added dimension of romance. Tell your mate what you like. Use a little body language. Nobody is a mind reader!

If you find it difficult to talk about the intimate side of your relationship, start by reading a book together. You may find that this is less threatening, and it may open the door for conversation—and who knows what doors conversation may open!

—*David and Claudia Arp*

Keeping Love Alive

*O*ne of the best ways to keep the imagination alive in your relationship is to be well-informed. Ask your friends how they add creativity to their marriages. Read books and magazines about subjects that would stimulate interesting conversation. My wife contributes so much to the variety of our marriage because she is constantly learning. She not only keeps her mind alert by reading, but she also takes courses on nutrition, gourmet cooking, and other special subjects. It seems she always has something new and interesting to talk about.

—Gary Smalley

*A*bove all, love each other deeply, because love covers over a multitude of sins.

—1 Peter 4:8

*D*on't forget that one of a husband's basic needs is admiration and respect. You'll never know how many points you can put in his Love Bank by slipping a note into his lunch or jacket pocket that says, "You're such a wonderful husband and such a great dad. The kids and I are so lucky that you belong to us."

—Dr. Kevin Leman

Ideas for Dating

Reminisce about the things during this past year that have drawn you closer together.

Address Christmas cards together and reminisce about the good times spent with those family members and friends.

Go to a bookstore and pick out a book for each other.

Attend a high school or college sporting event.

Try a Mexican restaurant for dinner.

Find a comfortable spot outside to lay back and watch the stars.

Make plans for a weekend trip.

Go to a French restaurant for dinner.

Bake and decorate a cake together.

Read poetry to each other.

*L*oving couples negotiate. They talk through something to find a mutually satisfying compromise. It's not that hard, really. You probably did it without thinking when you were dating and oh-so-willing to consider the other person's wishes.

Winston Churchill once said, "The English never draw a line without blurring it." That should be true of the couple who learns to compromise. When a husband and wife come to believe that equality means splitting things precisely down the middle, then marriage becomes a contest of who can get a better deal. And that wipes out the true spirit of compromise. Finding an agreeable solution to disagreements means that sometimes one or the other partner gets a bigger piece of the pie.

—Les and Leslie Parrott

It is love, not reason, that is stronger than death.

—*Thomas Mann*

*I*f you develop a positive attitude, not only will others want to be around you more often, but your wife will also benefit tremendously. She will have a greater sense of worth and value, knowing you have provided the encouragement only a husband can give.

Encourage your wife and deepen your marriage relationship by learning how to praise her. Promise yourself to tell your wife daily what you appreciate about her. Promise yourself— not her—because she might develop expectations and be hurt if you forget. Begin by learning to verbalize your thoughts of appreciation.

—*Gary Smalley*

A strong decision never to divorce will give safety and security to a relationship. It provides the marriage an environment for intimacy and bonding. But you need to take your commitment a step farther. When Roger and I got married more than twenty years ago, we decided to never use the "D" word: divorce. We felt that even using the word would be damaging to our relationship. We didn't want to open the door, even a crack, to let the thought enter our minds. We have kept our word. Closing the door to the very mention of divorce prevented us from even considering bailing out when difficult adjustments and personal differences surfaced. It forced us to search for ways to change, cope and grow. When we would otherwise choose to abandon, we choose to stay connected and work through our struggles.

—Dr. Roger and Becky Tirabassi

*E*very husband and every wife is different and has different ways of giving and receiving love. For some people touch is the primary language of love. Their spouse can say, "I love you" twenty times a day but without an embrace or a kiss or a squeeze they won't feel loved. Other people need to hear verbal expressions of love. They need to hear in concrete terms why their spouse loves them. Service is what makes some people feel most loved. They respond best to affection that is revealed in practical terms. Gifts make other people feel loved—not because of the cost involved, but because of the personal attention and thought that goes into them. Spending time together makes other people feel loved. They don't care particularly what they and their spouses do, as long as they are together.

—Bill and Lynne Hybels

Keeping Love Alive

*I*f I give all I possess to the poor and surrender my body to the flames, but have not love, I gain nothing.

—1 Corinthians 13:3

*S*trengthen me with raisins, refresh me with apples, for I am faint with love.

—Song of Songs 2:5

*W*omen need praise. We should be able to understand their need because we, too, want to know that we are of value to other people. One of the ways we know we're needed is when others express appreciation for who we are and what we do. When you praise your wife, it's important to use words and actions that communicate praise from her point of view. Anything that is romantic or deals with building deeper relationships usually pleases wives.

—Gary Smalley

Tips for Loving Him

Tell him how attractive he is.

Wash and powder or lotion his feet tonight.

Pray for him.

Write him a love letter for Valentine's Day.

Wash and vacuum his car.

Let him have "the guys" over.

Laugh with him, not at him.

Just be yourself.

Listen.

Tell him what is wrong.

Keeping Love Alive

Love is not blind. Love takes a good, hard look at reality. That's why love rejoices with the truth. Truth keeps love honest, reminding it that an untrustworthy person who is loved is still untrustworthy. Real love does not live in an idealistic fairy tale. It doesn't sweep unpleasant bits of reality under the rug. No. Love is open-eyed to what's really going on. It allows us to recognize the presence of evil when all we want to see is good. Sure, love softens the jagged corners of hard truths. It guards against the all-too-frequent brutality of reality. But love never loses sight of the way things really are.

—*Les and Leslie Parrott*

*W*herever you are in your marriage, don't take your spouse for granted. Keep looking forward. Keep forgiving and asking for forgiveness. Keep on being patient with each other. Let compassion and kindness flow from your life to the love of your life. Keep dreaming and being willing to let go of missed dreams and release those little disappointments.

Recommit yourself to your spouse and to your marriage. You can handle disappointments and move on in your marriage. You can reconnect and rebuild your relationship. You can refocus on your mate and in the process, become a loving and close companion.

—*David and Claudia Arp*

Keeping Love Alive

Tips for Loving Her

Let her sleep late on Saturday morning.

Massage her neck and shoulders.

Bring home a music tape you think she will enjoy.

Buy her a magazine she will enjoy reading.

Offer to take the kids out on Saturday.

Change the oil in her car.

Water her plants.

Put the toilet seat down.

Make a date for lunch.

Be nice to her mother.

$\mathcal{L}$ove does not brood over injuries. It keeps no record of wrongs because it cannot survive in doing so. Love knows that keeping track of tit for tat never brings equilibrium to an out-of-balance relationship. Love understands that wrongs are a part of life and that no record can ever right them. Instead, the power of love is found in letting go of our record keeping. It loosens our grip on past pain and drives us to a fresh start. Love lets the history die and gives birth to a new beginning. It surrenders the compulsion to clear up every misunderstanding and lets the ledgers stay unbalanced. Love prefers to let forgiveness heal former hurts so that we can focus on the future.

—*Les and Leslie Parrott*

Talk Together

Negotiate some quiet time for each of you when the other spouse is in charge of the children.

Decide on a budget for leisure time and vacation activities.

Share something interesting that you read this week.

Share with each other what your needs are in making love.

Discuss your hopes and dreams for the future.

Share what your favorite television show is and watch both of them together.

Evaluate your bedtime hour.

Talk about how you have felt when ex-boy or girlfriends have been brought up in conversations. Decide if you want to agree not to mention these people again.

Discuss how you feel about your spiritual growth as a couple.

Talk about people you would like to have over for a meal. Choose one person or family and invite them over in the coming week.

*M*ay the Lord make your love increase and overflow for each other and for everyone else.

—*1 Thessalonians 3:12*

*L*asting friendships are built in foxholes. Nothing binds two people together faster than a common struggle against the enemy. Virtually any crisis can draw you and your husband closer, whether it be a stopped-up sink or your unwed daughter's pregnancy. No one hunts for tragedy, but if it strikes at your door, you can strengthen your marriage by dealing with it as a team.

—*Gary Smalley*

I am my lover's and my lover is mine.

—*Song of Songs 6:3*

$\mathcal{W}$hoso loves believes the impossible.

—*Elizabeth Barrett Browning*

*E*mpathy is perhaps the toughest work of building a strong marriage. Because most of us are wired to use either our head or heart, one more than the other, it takes a conscious effort to empathize. Empathy, however, brings together both sympathetic and analytic abilities, both heart and head, to fully understand our partners. Empathy says, "If I were you, I would act as you do; I understand why you feel the way you feel."

Empathy always involves risk, so be forewarned. Accurately understanding your partner's hurts and hopes will change you—but the benefits of taking that risk far outweigh the disadvantages. Once you consciously feel his or her feelings and understand his or her perspective, you will see the world differently.

—*Les and Leslie Parrott*

Keeping Love Alive

$\mathcal{H}$e who covers over an offense promotes love.

—*Proverbs 17:9*

$\mathcal{L}$ife-long love does not happen by chance but is an art that must be learned, practiced, and honed.

—*Les and Leslie Parrott*

$\mathcal{R}$omance depends on your attitude and perspective. Too often we take ourselves and our mates too seriously. Or we always hurry. Remember, whatever you do to promote romance, getting there is half the fun. Making time for love will help you be good to each other. Take time to unwind from your busy day; make the transition slowly. Go for a walk and hold hands. Stop along the way for a kiss or two. Taking time to kiss and cuddle and laugh and share intimate thoughts during your lovemaking will add romance.

—*David and Claudia Arp*

*W*hen a husband and wife come together after an absence—upon waking, getting home from work, or returning from a trip—the first few minutes will set the stage for how the rest of the time will go. Family therapist Marcia Lasswell says, "It's very important that the first few minutes of reconnection be positive and supportive. We all know how good it feels to walk into someone's presence and have them look up and smile, and how awful it is if he or she is preoccupied or negative." We know this because the "it's-good-to-see-you" look is what we instinctively gave, and received, in the early stages of our dating relationship.

—Les and Leslie Parrott

Keeping Love Alive

$\mathcal{M}$any couples tying the knot today will have several different marriage partners over their lifetime. But it doesn't have to be that way! Not if we are willing to generously oil our relationships with love and forgiveness. All marriages need forgiveness and a big dose of reality. No spouse is perfect! Even when we are trying to please the other, we can mess up. We find that as we live out our love relationship daily, both of us need to forgive and ask the other for forgiveness. While we try to accept each other's little irritating habits, at times we react and need to ask for forgiveness.

—*David and Claudia Arp*

Tips for Loving Him

Write him a note. The key word is "Adore."

Pretend you think his old car is awesome.

Buy him his favorite candy.

Warm up the car for him on cold mornings.

Leave a message on his answering machine.

Leave notes in different pockets of his jeans.

Run an errand he hates to do.

Take him out for dinner.

Laugh at the jokes you've heard 10 times.

Believe in him.

*Don't mention his weight gain,
he already knows about it.*

Keeping Love Alive

*Y*ou probably weren't somber and sad when your husband married you. So, if you want to be his best friend now, you may need to add a little humor to your relationship. No need to buy a clown suit. Just look for ways to tickle his funny bone. Clip those comics or cartoons that strike you as funny and save them for his enjoyment during lighthearted times. Be willing to loosen up and laugh heartily when he tells a good joke. There are countless ways to add humor to your marriage. Be willing to set aside the serious quest for romance at times to enjoy just having fun together as friends.

—Gary Smalley

*E*very successful marriage is the result of two people
working diligently and skillfully to cultivate their love.
When they combine passion, intimacy, and commitment,
they are able to grow a flourishing, healthy marriage.

—*Les and Leslie Parrott*

A comfortable, orderly home which offers a peaceful
atmosphere makes for marital happiness. Creative clutter is
one thing; messiness which drives your partner (and you,
too) "up the wall" needs to be remedied. God, truly, is the
God of order, not of confusion. Many fine "help" books are
available to take you through this problem. When one
determines to keep a perfect house, that also can cause
discomfort and unhappiness. Your goal should be a home
you both can enjoy and the freedom to invite people into
your house without worrying about its "disaster area"
appearance.

—*Ed Wheat*

Keeping Love Alive

Spouses routinely underestimate the importance of a kind word. We're not talking about elaborate praise or a heartfelt poem, as wonderful as these things are. We're talking about the simple, everyday kindness of small talk. "Thanks." "You're great." "I missed you today."

Each of us needs someone to listen to the little everyday aspects of our life, like how irritated you were in the school parking lot or how friendly the person you met at the grocery store was. When you chime in with the occasional "uh huh" or "really?" you're showing that you care not just about the chitchat at hand, but about the speaker, your spouse. And that's good for the soul. It calms our anxious heart and cheers our heavy spirit.

—*Les and Leslie Parrott*

*H*usbands ought to love their wives as their own bodies. He who loves his wife loves himself.

—Ephesians 5:28

*T*he level of a couple's joy is determined by each partner's ability to adjust to things beyond his or her control. Every happy couple has learned to find the right attitude in spite of the conditions they find themselves in.

—Les and Leslie Parrott

*M*any women have told me about the importance of intimate communication with their husbands—special togetherness times—after the children are in bed, during the day on the telephone, at breakfast, at dinner, at a restaurant over a cup of coffee. These special sharing times can be the most enjoyable part of a woman's day.

—Gary Smalley

Ideas for Dating

Visit a pet shop and look for the most exotic pet.

Decorate your home with lights at Christmas.

Take an early spring bike ride.

Go to the movies and see a comedy. Laugh!

Look over new homes for features you both like.

Go to the florist and pick out a plant.

*Take a drive, and flip a penny at each crossroad
to determine which way to turn.*

Go fishing together.

*Take an early morning walk and enjoy
the outdoors together.*

Play a board game together.

Keeping Love Alive

*W*e recommend a weekend getaway. Nothing helps revive romance like focused time away together. If your budget is limited, be creative. Some couples trade houses and condos. Maybe you have adult children who would loan you their homes when they are away. When our oldest son and daughter-in-law lived in Williamsburg, Virginia, they offered us their apartment when they were going to be away for several weeks. Imagine our surprise when we arrived to find the table romantically set for two, with candles and their best china! Go on and think creatively. Plan a getaway for yourselves!

—David and Claudia Arp

$\mathcal{T}$o love at all is to be vulnerable.

—*C. S. Lewis*

Tips for Loving Her

Help her think beyond tomorrow.

Let her sleep late.

Plant a rose bush for her.

Scrub the floor.

Calm her fears.

Rub her feet.

Let her go out with her friends.

Brush the snow off her car.

Let her cry.

Clear a path to her car on a snowy morning.

Keeping Love Alive

$\mathcal{L}$isten! My lover! Look! Here he comes, leaping across the mountains, bounding over the hills. My lover is like a gazelle or a young stag. Look! There he stands behind our wall, gazing through the windows, peering through the lattice. My lover spoke and said to me, "Arise, my darling, my beautiful one, and come with me. See! The winter is past; the rains are over and gone. Flowers appear on the earth; the season of singing has come, the cooing of doves is heard in our land. The fig tree forms its early fruit; the blossoming vines spread their fragrance. Arise, come, my darling; my beautiful one, come with me."

—Song of Songs 2:8-13

*I*f you want to reclaim table time with your spouse, make it a pleasant time that both of you look forward to. You don't have to cook like Julia Child or set a table like Martha Stewart to make mealtimes pleasurable. What matters most is the focus of your conversation. Don't allow it to be a time of dumping your problems on your partner. When your spouse asks you how your day was, even if it was horrendous, say, "I'll tell you in a minute, but right now it's good to be home with you." Set the tone for an evening that will be uplifting, spontaneous, and positive. Give your partner your attention before you give him or her your problems.

—*Les and Leslie Parrott*

Just Do It

Enjoy a sunset together.

Take a walk and listen for birds singing.

Set up a schedule for meal preparations and kitchen chores you can do together.

Rearrange the living room furniture together.

Pack a snack and find a peaceful place to eat outdoors.

Call when you are going to be late.

Send a "thinking of you" e-mail message.

Give an unexpected hug.

Develop a sense of humor.

Be trustworthy.

Prefer her over others.

$\mathcal{H}$ave you ever thought of applying all you know about good manners and courtesy in your times of relating sexually? The purpose of etiquette is to smooth and improve human relations. Many sexual problems result from ignoring bedroom etiquette, and good manners in the sexual relationship could cure some of the dysfunctions we must treat.

The truly courteous are warm, kind, generous, and flexible in the bedroom. They consider one another's needs and feelings, and approach sex with their partner not as a right, but a privilege. Courtesy is made up of tact and foresight—looking ahead to see how what you say or do will affect another person. Tact means to touch delicately. As a considerate lover, you will try to relate to your loved one with this "delicacy of touch," and you will avoid being careless or rude in the name of relaxed intimacy.

—*Ed Wheat*

*L*et us not love with words or tongue but with actions and in truth.

—*1 John 3:18*

*M*arriage is not a machine that needs routine maintenance to keep it functioning, but a supernatural event founded upon a mutual exchange of holy pledges. Above all, marriage is a deep, mysterious, and unfathomable endeavor.

—*Les and Leslie Parrott*

*S*exual fulfillment that bonds the two of you in the forever relationship of marriage will include these elements: the assurance of being accepted and desired; the well-being that comes from intimate physical and emotional closeness; the sensuous delights of loving caresses; and the wonderful feeling of belonging to each other in the one-flesh relationship of God's devising.

—*Ed Wheat*

Tips for Staying Romantic

Try incorporating the following ingredients into your personal romantic style.

The element of the unexpected. Anything that is repeated month after month, year after year, can easily become humdrum.

The element of dating. Laugh and enjoy each other and be a little crazy.

The element of the impractical. Impractical romantic events create moments to remember.

The element of creativity. Discover what delights your partner and then make those delights happen in creative ways.

The element of the daily. Romance involves daily acts of care, concern, love, listening and giving each other your personal attention.

The element of commitment. If commitment to each other is at the heart of your marriage, romance will thrive.

—H. Norman Wright

Keeping Love Alive

$\mathcal{W}$e hope you will find time to pace yourself, to stoke your own fire, and make your love relationship a priority. Take it from our friends Dave and Jeanne: it can just keep getting better and better as the years go by. "Romance doesn't have to die out," said Dave. "It can grow and blossom through all your married years, if you continue to show your love in physical ways plus loving words and deeds. God designed man and woman to enjoy each other in marriage, and we find that enjoyment still growing after forty-five years of marriage."

Let us encourage you to fan the fires of romance. You never know where it might lead. Go on and take the risk. Stoke your own fire and enjoy your marriage with your lover and your best friend.

—David and Claudia Arp

Keeping Love Alive

*E*ach one of you also must love his wife as he loves himself, and the wife must respect her husband.

—Ephesians 5:33

*T*rue love transforms everything. As Richard McBrain states so elegantly: "Love is . . . at the heart of every other Christian virtue. Thus, for example, justice without love is legalism; faith without love is ideology; hope without love is self-centeredness; forgiveness without love is self-abasement; fortitude without love is recklessness; generosity without love is extravagance; care without love is mere duty; fidelity without love is servitude. Every virtue is an expression of love. No virtue is really a virtue unless it is permeated, or informed, by love."

—Les and Leslie Parrott

*T*hose who plan what is good find love and faithfulness.

—Proverbs 14:22

Enjoy Each Other

Remember what you first loved about each other.

Cuddle up and relive your first date. What would you want to be the same? What would you want to be different?

Go out and purchase the largest pumpkin you can find. Carve out the pumpkin and bake the pumpkin seeds for a snack later.

Visit a hobby shop and look for something you would enjoy doing together.

Stroll through the mall holding hands.

Get dressed up and go to a fancy restaurant with friends.

Check the newspaper to find a play or concert to attend.

Take an early morning walk and look for signs of the season changing.

Lay in front of the fire together and dream about the future.

*R*eplace a judgmental or faultfinding attitude with a positive response and a consistently accepting attitude and you will have the ideal climate for a loving interchange of thoughts and feelings. This can lead to the deepening of your love relationship. A young husband, who had been admittedly impatient and somewhat critical, told us, "I have become sensitive to Katie's reaction when I criticize or even show impatience. It seems to be a function of the love God has given me for her that now it hurts me so badly when I see her hurt that I have to back off." He's learning the secret: Good communication begins with acceptance.

—*Ed Wheat*

$\mathcal{T}$ake away love and our
earth is a tomb.

—*Robert Browning*

*T*he ideal day of romance, according to survey results, included breakfast in bed, a picnic in the country, or an elegant dinner. Jacuzzis figured prominently in the response. So did the element of surprise and the absence of interruptions. One woman said her ideal day of romance was simple: "He'd never call his office or take calls on his portable phone."

The message is clear, men. We don't have to be a Mel Gibson or a Brad Pitt to make love exciting. We don't have to spend money like Donald Trump to be romantic. Women admire enduring love over all-consuming passion, time and again. They aren't looking for expensive preprogrammed evenings. They'll take the spontaneous heartfelt gesture of love every time.

—Les and Leslie Parrott

Keeping Love Alive

*I*f there is anything that kills romance, it is sameness. Every married couple experiences the "letdown" that follows the first glow and breathlessness of falling in love, tying the knot, and then discovering that reality seems to leave out romance. But it doesn't have to be that way if you are both committed to keeping each other off balance with little surprises that say in different ways, "I love you," "I'm proud of you," "I really like being married to you!" and sometimes the surprises can be big ones—wild and crazy stuff, perhaps, or just taking time to make a date or a weekend a lot more special and intimate.

—*Dr. Kevin Leman*

$\mathcal{T}$he foundation of willpower is a set of marital promises.
It is this set of promises that serves as the steel structure of
every great marriage. Marriage doesn't just happen! It takes
a solid set of decisions, a huge amount of skill, and enormous
willpower. I contend that people in extremely healthy
marriages built those marriages just as you build a mammoth
bridge or a skyscraper. They made their marriage triumphant
because they simply wouldn't settle for less. It doesn't matter
at all to them how much backbreaking work it requires; if it
were necessary, they would do a thousand times more. Their
willpower gives them this kind of toughness.

—*Dr. Neil Clark Warren*

*Y*ou can shower your partner with love, but if you're not real, the love is hollow. You can use all the communication techniques in the world, but if you aren't genuine, they won't work. Authenticity is something you are, not something you do. It comes from the heart, not the hands.

—*Les and Leslie Parrott*

*T*o love your wife responsibly means nothing less than putting her ahead of yourself as you look out for her best interests and highest welfare.

—*Ed Wheat*

*C*ommunicate with one purpose in mind: To learn how to be a better marriage partner. Stay away from should-ing, ought-ing, always-ing, and never-ing each other. I like the way Willard Harley puts it: "An intimate conversation cannot include an argument."

—*Dr. Kevin Leman*

Tips for Loving Her

Pretend you like her cat.

Put her favorite candy bar in her purse.

Hold hands in public.

Take out the garbage without being asked.

Share her dreams.

Give her time to herself.

Tell her she's not getting older, just better.

Notice what she is wearing and compliment her.

Tell her you are glad you married her.

Treat her as an intellectual equal.

Buy her what she considers an intimate gift.

*G*ive your working wife emotional support. Listen to her without offering quick advice—just listen with understanding and sympathy. Encourage her! Remember that as a woman she is much more apt to blame herself when things go wrong at work. Since she tends to be more subjective and sensitive in her dealings with supervisors and co-workers than you, she will probably suffer more acutely than you when things get out of order in her home—for a woman's house is an extension of herself, whether she has time to give to its care or not.

—*Ed Wheat*

*H*usbands and wives need to consider what they say in an effort to be honest. The tongue should be a monitor, rather than an open channel, of our thoughts. Perhaps we can't keep hurtful thoughts from coming into our minds, but we can refuse to speak those thoughts that might bring pain to another.

In a healthy marriage, you can tell your spouse anything, but you aren't obligated to tell your spouse everything. Whenever you wonder whether to tell your spouse something, stop and ask who will benefit if you share it. A tongue that speaks the truth in love—rather than total honesty about every feeling that you have—is the surest route to intimacy in marriage.

—Jeanette and Robert Lauer

Tips for Better Communication

Express your feelings and frustrations honestly, without accusing or attacking.

Choose words, expressions and a tone of voice that are kind and gentle.

Do not exaggerate, distort or stretch the truth. Avoid extreme words like "never" and "always."

Give specific examples; stay away from generalities.

Seek solutions rather than merely airing grievances.

Listen to what your spouse is saying, feeling and needing.

Refuse to indulge bitterness, anger, withdrawal or argument.

Acknowledge your own failure, and don't hesitate to forgive.

Keep communicating until you both understand what the other is saying and feeling.

Train your mouth and heart to say the right thing at the right time in the right way for the right reason.

—*Gary and Betsy Ricucci*

Keeping Love Alive

Virtually every couple who takes the marriage vows fully intends to fulfill them. On their wedding day, most couples are not thinking of the "poorer" and "worse" and "sickness" parts of their vows. They're filled with hopes, dreams, and expectations. Eventually, of course, reality sets in, and they begin to live out the final phrase of the vows—sticking together until death parts them. That's when marriage gets dicey. That's when marriage needs protection.

Our society is full of people whose dreams of lifelong commitment have been shattered. But those who take their wedding vows seriously believe that a promise is made to be kept, till death. That promise is made not only with their heads, but also with their hearts.

—*Les and Leslie Parrott*

Ideas for Dating

Pack a basket with a healthy dinner and go to a park for a picnic.

Assemble and wrap your Christmas packages together.

Go to the lake shore and walk barefoot in the sand.

Organize your vacation pictures and write captions for them.

Share an early morning breakfast on a Saturday morning at a local restaurant to make the weekend seem longer.

Over coffee at your favorite bookstore, discuss the best book you have ever read.

Rent a sports car for the weekend and go for a long ride.

Play Scrabble together.

Watch the sunset—from your front porch or from a hilltop.

Go to a driving range and hit a bucket of golf balls.

⭐

*A*ffection, in the form of touching, is not only a preliminary to making love; it is a language that speaks more eloquently than words.

—*Les and Leslie Parrott*

*I*f you had only five minutes to express your appreciation to your spouse, what would you say to him or her? Reflect on your spouse's character qualities, achievements, skills and talents, and the special things he or she does for you. Then write your thoughts down. When you have completed your list, consider putting it in the form of a letter or poem and give it to your spouse. Or keep your list and use it to give your mate one honest compliment each day in the coming week.

—*David and Claudia Arp*

$\mathcal{T}$his is the true measure of love, when
we believe that we alone can love, that
no one could ever have loved so before
us, and that no will ever love in the
same way after us.

—*Johann Wolfgang von Goethe*

*B*eing married changes us, not because being changed is our goal, but because of who we are in relationship with. When someone truly loves and accepts you, your defenses go down and you're more likely to change.

—*Will Willimon*

*J*acob was in love with Rachel and said, "I'll work for you seven years in return for your younger daughter Rachel." Laban said, "It's better that I give her to you than to some other man. Stay here with me." So Jacob served seven years to get Rachel, but they seemed like only a few days to him because of his love for her.

—*Genesis 29:18-20*

*I*f a holy God can bear with us in spite of our daily transgressions, why can't we extend to each other a larger dose of mercy and acceptance? No matter how frustrated we may become with our spouse, approaching each other with open arms—rather than anger or silence—presents a clearer picture of God's patience with each of us.

—*Ron and Jeanette Lee*

Tips for Loving Him

Buy him that "toy" you know he wants.

Clean out his car.

Buy his favorite ice cream rather than yours.

Frost a big chocolate chip cookie with "I Love You."

Be his best friend.

Care about what has happened in his day.

Mow the lawn for him.

Put his sports trophies on display.

Accept him as he is. Don't ask him to change.

Tell his friends how wonderful he is.

*H*ow then do a man and a woman become one in marriage? To put it another way: How do a man and a woman become soul mates? The answer is found exactly where you might suspect—deep in the soul. Recently scientific research has backed up what common sense has been telling us for years; mainly, that tending to the spiritual dimension of marriage is what unites couples in unbreakable bonds. Marriage thrives when its soul is nourished.

Tending the soul of your marriage requires constant attention. For if you neglect the soul of your marriage there will be only superficial bonding, which rides the waves of emotion and infatuation until the marriage is beached. But if in your sojourn together you tend the soul—through worship, service, and prayer—you will make it through the storms of marriage unscathed.

—Les and Leslie Parrott

$\mathcal{T}$he greatest happiness of life is the
conviction that we are loved . . .
loved for ourselves, or rather,
loved in spite of ourselves.

—*Victor Hugo*

Sources

100 Ways to Say I Love You. Grand Rapids, MI: Zondervan Publishing House, 1993.

Arp, David and Claudia. *The Second Half of Marriage.* Grand Rapids, MI: Zondervan Publishing House, 1996.

Couple's Devotional Bible. Grand Rapids, MI: Zondervan Publishing House, 1994.

Crabb, Larry, et al. *Bring Home the Joy.* Grand Rapids, MI: Zondervan Publishing House, 1998.

Hybels, Bill and Lynne. *Fit to Be Tied.* Grand Rapids, MI: Zondervan Publishing House, 1993.

Parrott, Drs. Les and Leslie. *Like a Kiss on the Lips.* Grand Rapids, MI: Zondervan Publishing House, 1997.

Parrott, Drs. Les and Leslie. *Love is . . .* Grand Rapids, MI: Zondervan Publishing House, 1999.

Parrott, Drs. Les and Leslie. *Saving Your Marriage Before It Starts.* Grand Rapids, MI: Zondervan Publishing House, 1995.

Richards, Larry and Sue. *Keeping Your Love Alive.* Grand Rapids, MI: Zondervan Publishing House, 1996.

Smalley, Gary. *For Better or for Best.* Grand Rapids, MI: Zondervan Publishing House, 1979.

Smalley, Gary. *The Joy of Committed Love.* Grand Rapids, MI: Zondervan Publishing House, 1984.

Warren, Neil Clark, Ph.D. *Learning to Live with the Love of Your Life and Loving It!* (formerly published under the title *The Triumphant Marriage*,) a Focus on the Family book published by Tyndale House. Copyright © 1995 by Neil Clark Warren, Ph.D.

Wheat, Ed. *The First Years of Forever.* Grand Rapids, MI: Zondervan Publishing House, 1988.